Pork

Cookbook

Table of Contents

Introduction

If you are looking for the perfect entrée that is a definite crowd pleaser, you can't go wrong with serving pork chops. Pork chops are naturally lean and incredibly versatile.

They can be stuffed, fried, breaded or grilled. When people think of lean meats they often think of chicken, but pork chops are a delicious option that are sure to please everyone. This cookbook is full of tasty recipes from smokey to savory to sweet. There is something for everyone.

Skillet Pork Chops

Pork Chops and Apples

Isn't that swell!

Ingredients:

4 pork chops
1 (16 oz.) can sauerkraut
1 onion, chopped
1 Tbl. Packed brown sugar
3 medium russet potatoes, peeled, cut
1 (10 oz.) can cream of mushroom soup
1 red apple.

Directions:

1. Peel and core apple and cut in to wedges.
2. Peel potatoes and cut in to ½ inch cubes.
3. Brown pork chops on both sides on medium high heat in a skillet.
4. Remove chops and set aside.
5. Preheat oven to 350 degrees F.
6. Add undrained sauerkraut, onion and brown sugar to skillet.
7. Sauté for about 5 minutes.
8. Spoon into a lightly greased baking dish.
9. Arrange pork chops on top of sauerkraut mixture.
10. Place potatoes around edges of baking dish.
11. Spread undiluted soup over chops.
12. Arrange apple wedges around chops.
13. Bake, covered for 20 minutes or until potatoes are almost tender.
14. Bake, uncovered, until pork is cooked through and potatoes are tender, about 10 minutes.

Apricot-Glazed Pork Chops

Ingredients:

4 boneless pork chops
1/2 tsp. salt
1/4 tsp. pepper
2 Tbl. Vegetable oil
1/2 cup apricot nectar
1/4 cup soy sauce
1 clove garlic, minced
1/3 cup apricot preserves
2 cups hot cooked white rice.

Directions:

1. Sprinkle pork with salt and pepper.
2. Heat oil in a large skillet over medium high heat.
3. Add pork to skillet.
4. Cook until browned on both sides, turning once, about 10 minutes.
5. Combine nectar, soy sauce, garlic and preserves in a small bowl.
6. Mix well.
7. Pour apricot mixture over pork.
8. Reduce heat.
9. Simmer, covered, until pork is cooked through, about 20 minutes.
10. Serve over hot rice.

Pork Chops with Cranberry Sauce

Ingredients:

6 pork chops (smoked is best)
1 (16 oz. can whole cranberry sauce
1 (10 oz.) can tomato soup
1 envelope onion soup mix
2 cups water
1/2 tsp. salt
1/2 tsp. ground ginger
1 tbsp. chopped red bell pepper
1 cup white rice
1/4 cup frozen green peas, thawed

Directions:

1. Preheat oven to 350 degrees F.
2. Spray a large skillet with cooking spray.
3. Cook pork chops over medium high heat until tightly browned on both sides, about 3 minutes.
4. Arrange pork chops in a large baking dish.
5. Combine cranberry sauce, tomato soup and soup mix in a saucepan.
6. Cook, stirring occasionally, over medium heat until warm.
7. Pour over pork and cover.
8. Bake for about 40 minutes.
9. Combine water, salt, ginger and bell pepper in a medium saucepan.
10. Stir in rice.
11. Bring to a boil.
12. Reduce heat and cook covered until rice is tender (about 15 minutes)
13. Remove from heat and stir in peas.
14. Let stand, covered for 5 minutes.
15. Serve pork chops and sauce over rice.

Thai Pork Chops

Ingredients:

1 tbsp. olive oil
4 center-cut pork rib chops, 1/2-inch thick
2 red jalapeno chiles, seeded, finely chopped
2 garlic cloves, finely chopped
1/4 cup fish sauce
4 tsp. sugar
1/4 cup chopped cilantro
1/4 cup chopped dry roasted nuts

Directions:

1. Heat oil in lg skillet over medium high heat.
2. Add pork chops, cook 8-10 min, turning once.
3. Add chilies and garlic, cook over medium heat 1-2 min or until softened.
4. Stir occasionally.
5. Stir in fish sauce and sugar, bring to boil.
6. Boil 1 minute.
7. Pour over pork chops.
8. Sprinkle with cilantro and peanuts.

Sesame Glazed Pork Chops

Ingredients:

2 tbsp. sesame seeds
1/2 tsp. salt
1/4 tsp. pepper
4 (6 oz.) pork chops, about 1" thick
2 tsp. dark sesame oil
1/2 cup chicken broth
1 tbsp. brown sugar
2 tbsp. red wine vinegar
1 tbsp. Dijon mustard

Directions:

1. Heat a small skillet over medium-high heat.
2. Add sesame seeds.
3. Cook, stirring until seeds are golden (about 2 minutes).
4. Remove from skillet.
5. Sprinkle salt and pepper over pork chops.
6. Heat oil in a medium skillet over medium-high heat.
7. Add pork chops.
8. Cook pork chops for 3 minutes on each side.
9. Add broth, brown sugar, vinegar, mustard and sesame seeds.
10. Stir to mix well.
11. Reduce heat to low.
12. Cook, covered for 15 minutes.
13. Uncover skillet.
14. Cook until pork chops are tender, about 15 minutes longer.
15. Serve pork chops with sauce.

Balsamic Honey Glazed Pork Chops

Ingredients:

2 pork loin chops
olive oil
salt and pepper
2 cloves garlic, crushed
2 tbsp. honey
1/2 cup balsamic vinaigrette dressing

Directions:

1. Heat enough olive oil to lightly coat your frying pan.
2. Heat oil on medium high heat.
3. Crush the cloves of garlic and rub on pork chops both sides, add salt and pepper to taste.
4. Add pork chops to the heated oil.
5. Brown pork chop on each side (about 2 minutes per side).
6. Once browned, reduce heat to medium low.
7. Add the balsamic vinaigrette and honey to the frying pan.
8. Coat the pork chop in the sauce and simmer for 10 min.

Sweet Barbecued Pork Chops

Ingredients:

2 tbsps. canola oil
6 boneless pork loin chops
1/2 cup packed brown sugar
1/2 cup chopped sweet onion
1/2 cup ketchup,
1/2 cup barbecue sauce
1/2 cup French salad dressing
1/2 cup honey

Directions:

1. In a large skillet, heat oil over medium heat, brown the pork chops 2-3 minutes on each side.
2. Return all the pork chops to the pan.
3. In a small bowl, mix remaining ingredients.
4. Pour over chops.
5. Bring to a boil then reduce heat.
6. Simmer, covered for about 4-5 minutes.
7. Let stand 5 minutes before serving.
8. Enjoy!

Homestyle Pork Chops

Ingredients:

1 tsp. McCormick® Paprika
1/2 tsp. McCormick® Thyme Leaves
1/2 tsp. salt
1/4 tsp. McCormick® Black Pepper, Ground
4 bone-in pork chops, 1/2-inch thick
1 tbsp. olive oil

Directions:

1. Mix paprika, thyme, salt and black pepper in small bowl.
2. Sprinkle evenly over both sides of pork chops.
3. Heat oil in large nonstick skillet on medium heat.
4. Add pork chops.
5. Cook 4 minutes per side or until desired doneness.

Steakhouse Pork Chops

Ingredients:

4 bone-in pork chops
Pepper to taste
Seas salt to taste
2 tsps. olive oil
1/4 cup balsamic vinegar

Directions:

1. Season each side of pork chops with 8 to 10 twists of a peppercorn grinder.
2. Heat oil in large skillet on medium heat.
3. Add pork chops.
4. Cook 5 to 6 minutes per side or until desired doneness.
5. Remove pork chops from skillet.
6. Stir vinegar into pan, scraping bottom to loosen browned bits. Serve sauce over pork chops.
7. Season to taste with sea salt.

Pork Chops Florentine

Ingredients:

6 loin pork chops, 1/2 to 3/4 inch thick
1 1/2 lb. fresh spinach, washed, chopped and lightly steamed
2 tbsp. butter
6 tbsp. flour
1 1/2 cup strong chicken stock
1 3/44 cup milk
Salt and pepper to taste
Dash of nutmeg
2 egg yolks, beaten lightly
1 cup grated Swiss cheese
3 tbsp. freshly grated Parmesan cheese

Directions:

1. Brown pork chops in lightly greased skillet. Lower heat.
2. Cover and cook about 30 minutes until tender. Keep warm.
3. Combine cooked spinach with the grated onion and set aside. In medium saucepan melt butter.
4. Stir in flour and cook over low heat for 3 minutes. Slowly stir in chicken stock and milk and continue to stir until thickened.
5. Add salt, pepper, and nutmeg.
6. Stir a little of the sauce into egg yolks and then return the yolk mixture to the sauce, stirring until smooth and thick.
7. Mix 1 cup sauce with spinach mixture and spread it over bottom of large, greased shallow casserole.
8. Arrange pork chops on top of spinach.
9. Meanwhile, stir Swiss cheese into sauce and stir over low heat until cheese is melted.
10. Pour over pork chops.
11. Sprinkle with Parmesan cheese and bake uncovered at 400 degrees for 15 minutes or until bubbling and cheese is lightly browned.

Pork Chops Marinara

Ingredients:

1 tbsp. vegetable oil
4 bone-in pork chops about 1" thick
1/2 tsp. salt
1 (28 oz.) can whole tomatoes
1/3 cup olive oil
3 cloves garlic, halved
1 tsp. sugar
1/2 tsp. fennel seeds
1 tbsp. dried seeds
1 tbsp. dried parsley

Directions:

1. Heat oil in a large skillet over a medium high heat.
2. Season pork chops with salt.
3. Cook for 2 minutes on each side.
4. Reduce heat to low.
5. Cook, covered for 5 minutes longer.
6. Remove pork chops from skillet.
7. Add tomatoes with liquid, oil, garlic, sugar, fennel, basil and parsley to skillet.
8. Cook over medium high heat, stirring.
9. Reduce heat to medium.
10. Cook until sauce is thickened, about 15 minutes.
11. Pour sauce into a blender or food processor.
12. Process briefly to break up tomato chunks.
13. Return sauce to skillet.
14. Add pork chops.
15. Heat until pork is warmed through, about 5 minutes.

Pork Chops And Spanish Rice

Ingredients:

4 pork chops
1 cup rice (white or brown long cooking)
2 tbsp. cooking oil
1 med. onion, chopped
1/4 cup chopped bell pepper
3 oz. tomato sauce
1 jalapeno or serrano pepper, chopped (optional)

Directions:

1. Season to taste with garlic salt, cayenne and black pepper
2. Enough boiling water to cook rice
3. In heavy skillet, brown seasoned pork chops and set aside. In second (or cleaned skillet, if same skillet is used) pour the cooking oil, heat on medium heat, and add rice.
4. Stir rice until it loses its translucency and puffs (not until it turns brown, although a few pieces may be brown).
5. Stir in onion and peppers, then tomato sauce to which the spices have been added. Lay pork chops on top of rice mixture; add boiling water.
6. Cover and cook until the water has been absorbed and the rice is done.
7. Add more boiling water if necessary.

Parmesan-Crusted Pork Chops

Ingredients:

2 large eggs
1 cup dried Italian-style bread crumbs
3/4 cups freshly grated Parmesan
4 pork chops
Salt and freshly ground black pepper
6 tbsp. olive oil

Directions:

1. Whisk the eggs in a shallow bowl.
2. Place the bread crumbs in another shallow bowl.
3. Place the cheese in a third shallow bowl.
4. Sprinkle the pork chops generously with salt and pepper.
5. Dip the pork chops in the cheese first, both sides, then pat it to get the cheese to adhere.
6. Dip the chops into the eggs next, both sides.
7. Dip the chops in the bread crumbs last, patting to adhere.
8. Heat 3 tbsps. of oil in a very large skillet over medium heat.
9. Cook pork chops in the skillet, in batches if necessary, until golden brown, about 6 minutes per side.
10. Serve and enjoy!

Barbecued Pork Chops

Ingredients:

6 (1 inch) pork chops
Salt and pepper
1 cup seasoned tomato sauce
1/2 cup catsup
1 tsp. Worcestershire
1 tsp. liquid smoke
1/2 tsp. onion salt

Directions:

1. Brown pork chops in heavy skillet with 2 tbsps. olive oil.
2. Season with salt and pepper.
3. Add all other ingredients and simmer 45-60 minutes, turning occasionally.

Pecan Crusted Pork Chops

Ingredients:

4 thick cut boneless pork chops
1.5 cups chopped pecans
1/4 cup breadcrumbs
1/4 cup honey mustard
1 egg
1/2 cup milk
1/2 cup vegetable oil for pan frying
Salt to taste

Directions:

1. Preheat oven to 350 F and prepare a sheet pan lined with parchment paper.
2. Prepare two shallow bowls or containers for breading the pork chops.
3. Combine the pecans and breadcrumbs in one, then whisk together the milk and eggs in another.
4. Working one chop at a time, season on both sides with salt, then spread 1 tbsp. of mustard along one side. Dip the chop into the egg mixture, allowing excess to drip off, then transfer to pecan mixture. Press the pecans in firmly to form a crust.
5. Repeat until all chops are crusted.
6. Place the oil into a skillet and heat over medium flame.
7. Fry the pork chops for a minute or two per side to develop color, being careful that the pecans do not burn.
8. Place browned chops on sheet pan and put the pan into the oven to finish cooking the chops. You may have to complete this step in two batches depending on the size of your skillet.
9. The chops are done when they reach an internal temperature of 145f, which will take about 15 minutes depending on thickness.

Pork Chop And Yellow Squash Skillet

Ingredients:

2 lbs. center cut pork chops
3-4 yellow squash, washed and sliced
1 (8 oz.) can tomato sauce
1/2 onion, chopped
2 tsp. garlic salt
Pepper

Directions:

1. Cut pork chops into bite size pieces.
2. Cook thoroughly in small amount of oil.
3. Add onion; cook until onion is tender.
4. Now add tomato sauce which has been mixed with 8 oz. water.
5. Liquid should cover ingredients, add water if necessary.
6. Season with garlic salt and black pepper.
7. Add squash and cover; simmer 30 minutes.
8. Serve with mashed potatoes, no gravy is needed.

Caribbean Pork Chops

Ingredients:

1 tbsp. Caribbean Jerk Seasoning
4 bone-in pork chops, 1/2-inch thick
1 tbsp. oil

Directions:

1. Sprinkle Seasoning evenly over both sides of pork chops.
2. Heat oil in large skillet on medium heat.
3. Add pork chops.
4. Cook 4 minutes per side or until desired doneness.

Fennel Crusted Pork Chops

Ingredients:

1 1/2 tbsps. fennel seeds
2 garlic cloves, finely grated
1 tsp. hot smoked Spanish paprika
3 tbsps. vegetable oil, divided
2 1"-thick bone-in pork loin chops
Kosher salt, freshly ground pepper
1 pound small Yukon Gold potatoes, quartered
2 large shallots, cut into quarters with some root attached
1/2 cup fresh flat-leaf parsley leaves
2 tsps. red wine vinegar

Directions:

1. Preheat oven to 450 degrees F. Toast fennel seeds in a small dry skillet over medium heat, tossing often, until fragrant, about 4 minutes. Let cool.
2. Combine fennel seeds, garlic, paprika, and 2 tbsps. oil in a small bowl.
3. Season pork with salt and pepper and place in a resealable plastic bag.
4. Add spice mixture; seal bag and turn to coat. Let sit at least 30 minutes.
5. Heat remaining 1 tbsp. oil in a large ovenproof skillet, preferably cast iron, over medium-high heat.
6. Cook pork chops until golden brown on 1 side, about 4 minutes; turn.
7. Add potatoes and shallots to skillet; season with salt and pepper and toss to coat in pan drippings.
8. Cook, tossing potatoes and shallots occasionally, until pork is golden brown on second side, about 4 minutes.
9. Transfer to oven and roast until potatoes are tender and an instant-read thermometer inserted into thickest part of chops registers 135 degrees F, 10–15 minutes. (If potatoes need more time, transfer chops to a plate and continue to roast potatoes until tender; transfer chops back to skillet when potatoes are done.) Remove skillet from oven and mix in parsley and vinegar. Let pork chops rest 5 minutes in skillet.
10. Transfer chops to a cutting board; cut meat from bones and slice against the grain. Serve with potatoes, shallots, and any pan juices.

Almond Crusted Pork Chops

Ingredients:

1 cup roasted salted almonds
3-4 6 oz. pork chops
2 egg whites
4 tbsp. avocado or olive oil divided
10 oz. sliced bella or white button mushrooms
4 cloves garlic
1 tbsp. arrowroot starch or your choice of thickening agent
1/2 dry white wine such as chardonnay or chicken broth
2 tbsp. white wine vinegar
Salt and Pepper to taste

Directions:

1. Begin by heating a large skillet to medium-medium high heat. Coat pan with 2 tbsp avocado oil or olive oil.
2. Prepare your pork chops: pulse almonds in a food processor or blender for 5-10 seconds (ensure that it doesn't become almond flour and over pulsed). Set aside almonds in a shallow dish. Now whisk together the egg whites and set aside in a separate bowl.
3. Place pork chops in the egg white mixture first, then move it to the almond mixture completely covering all sides of your pork chop.
4. Place inside your skillet and cook 4-6 minutes per side (this will depend on the thickness of your pork chops). Do not overcook!! They can be the slightest pink on the inside, but internal temperature should be 165 degrees.
5. Remove from the pan and set aside on a plate. Return your pan back to the burner. Turn the burner to medium.
6. Now make your sauce. Use the additional 2 tbsp avocado or olive oil and scrape up any residual almond mixture.
7. Toss in garlic and let saute for 1 minute, then add in mushrooms. Saute both the mushrooms and garlic and continue to stir for about 5 minutes, or until mushrooms are softened and flavored. Coat the mushrooms with arrowroot starch and continue to cook for another minute, stirring frequently. Now pour in wine and chicken broth. Increase heat to a boil, then reduce to low. let simmer for another 3-4 minutes or until liquid has thickened.
8. Add the pork chops back to the skillet to keep hot, and serve immediately generously pouring sauce over the pork chops. Serve with potatoes, vegetables, zoodles, or rice.

Vietnamese Pork Chops

Ingredients:

1 small shallot, finely chopped
1/3 cup (packed) light brown sugar
1/4 cup fish sauce
2 tbsps. unseasoned rice vinegar
1 tsp. freshly ground black pepper
4 1" thick pork chops
1 tbsp. vegetable oil
Kosher salt
Lime halves (for serving)

Directions:

1. Whisk shallot, brown sugar, fish sauce, vinegar, and pepper in a shallow dish.
2. Set aside some marinade for dipping before adding the pork chops.
3. Using a fork, pierce pork chops all over.
4. Add pork chops to remainder of marinade in dish.
5. Turn to coat.
6. Cover and let pork chops marinate at room temperature, turning occasionally for 20 minutes.
7. Remove pork chops from marinade, scraping off excess (reserve marinade for sauce).
8. Heat oil in a large skillet over medium-high heat.
9. Lightly season pork chops with salt.
10. Cook until browned and cooked through, about 4 minutes per side.
11. Let pork chops rest 10 minutes before serving.
12. Meanwhile, bring marinade to a boil in a small saucepan and cook until reduced to 1/4 cup, about 4 minutes.
13. Serve pork chops with reduced marinade and lime halves.

Pretzel-Crusted Pork

Ingredients:

4 cups apple cider
1 tbsp. light brown sugar
1 tbsp. kosher salt, plus more
4 (4-oz.) boneless pork chops or cutlets, pounded to 1/8" thickness
6 oz. pretzels
4 large eggs, beaten
1/3 cup whole grain mustard
3/4 cup all-purpose flour
Freshly ground black pepper
3 cups vegetable oil for frying
Sea salt

Directions:

1. Bring apple cider, brown sugar, and 1 tbsp. kosher salt to a boil in a medium saucepan and cook until reduced by half, 10–15 minutes.
2. Transfer to a shallow dish and let cool.
3. Add pork, cover, and chill at least 6 hours.
4. Pulse pretzels in a food processor to coarse crumbs.
5. Transfer to a shallow bowl.
6. Whisk eggs, mustard, and 2 Tbsp. water in another shallow bowl.
7. Place flour in a third shallow bowl.
8. Remove pork from brine, pat dry, and season with kosher salt and pepper.
9. Working one at a time, dip in flour, shaking off excess.
10. Dip into egg mixture, letting excess drip back into bowl.
11. Coat with pretzel crumbs, pressing firmly to adhere.
12. Pour oil into a large skillet to a depth of 1/2".
13. Heat over medium-high heat until it bubbles when a pinch of flour is added.
14. Working in batches, fry pork until golden brown and cooked through, about 2 minutes per side.
15. Drain on paper towels.
16. Season with sea salt.
17. Serve and enjoy!

Coffee Crusted Pork Chops

Ingredients:

4 bone-in, thick-cut pork chops (6 to 8 oz. each)
kosher salt, to taste
Fresh ground black pepper, to taste
4 tbsps. freshly ground coffee
1 tsps. brown sugar
2 tbsps. paprika
1 tbsp. chile powder
2 tsps. garlic powder
2 tsps. onion powder

Directions:

1. In a small bowl mix the coffee, brown sugar, paprika, chile powder, garlic powder and onion powder.
2. Season the pork chops with salt & pepper, then cover with ground coffee mixture.
3. Preheat oven to 450 degrees F. Heat oil over medium-high heat in a large oven-proof skillet.
4. Cook pork chops until beginning to brown, 3-4 minutes.
5. Turn and cook until second side is beginning to brown, about 2 minutes.
6. Keep turning chop every 2 minutes until both sides are deep golden brown, 10-12 minutes total.
7. Transfer skillet to oven and roast chops, about 15 minutes, turning every 2 minutes to prevent them from browning too quickly, until an instant-read thermometer inserted horizontally into center of meat registers 135°. The pork chop will continue to cook when it's resting.

Country Style Pork Chops

Ingredients:

1 egg, lightly beaten
1/2 cup milk
1-1/2 cups crushed saltine crackers
6 pork chops
1/4 cup canola oil

Directions:

1. In a shallow bowl, combine egg and milk.
2. Place cracker crumbs in another shallow bowl.
3. Dip each pork chop in egg mixture, then coat with cracker crumbs, patting to make a thick coating.
4. In a large skillet, cook chops in oil for 4-5 minutes on each side or until done.
5. Let stand for about 5 minutes before serving.

Cinnamon-Apple Pork Chops

Ingredients:

2 tbsps. reduced-fat butter, divided
4 boneless pork loin chops (4 oz. each)
3 tbsps. brown sugar
1 tsp. ground cinnamon
1/2 tsp. ground nutmeg
1/4 tsp. salt
4 medium tart apples, thinly sliced
2 tbsps. chopped pecans

Directions:

1. In a large skillet, heat 1 tbsp. butter over medium heat.
2. Add pork chops; cook 4-5 minutes on each side or until done.
3. In a small bowl, mix brown sugar, cinnamon, nutmeg and salt.
4. Remove pork chops and set aside.
5. Add apples, pecans, brown sugar mixture and remaining butter to pan.
6. Stir until apples are tender.
7. Serve with the pork chops.
8. Serve and enjoy!

Mushroom Gravy Pork Chops

Ingredients:

4 pork chops
3/4 cup all-purpose flour
1 tsp. onion powder
1 tsp. paprika
1/2 tsp. salt pepper to taste
3 tbsps. olive oil
3 tbsps. butter
3 cups sliced baby portebella mushrooms
1 small onion, sliced
3 cloves garlic, minced
1/4 cup all-purpose flour
11/2 cups beef broth
1/4 cup heavy cream

Directions:

1. Heat the 3 tbsp. of olive oil in a large skillet over medium low heat.
2. In a shallow dish combine the flour, onion powder, paprika, salt and pepper.
3. Dip each pork chop in the flour mixture and add to hot skillet.
4. Cook pork chops until golden brown on each side and juices are starting to run clear.
5. Remove from skillet and set aside.
6. Melt the butter in the skillet and add in the mushrooms and onions.
7. Cook until tender then add in the garlic and cook until fragrant.
8. Lightly season with salt and pepper.
9. Add in the 1/4 cup flour and stir to combine with the mushrooms and onion.
10. Slowly stir in the beef broth and cream, scraping the bits from the pan as you go.
11. Bring up to a simmer and add the pork chops back in.
12. Simmer on low heat for 3-5 minutes.
13. Serve and enjoy!

Butter Schnitzel

Ingredients:

12 boneless pork loin chops, 3/4 inch thick
2 cups bread crumbs
2 tbsps. grated Parmesan cheese
1 tbsp. dried parsley flakes
1 tsp. salt
1/2 tsp. freshly ground pepper
1/2 lb. butter
2 cloves garlic, minced
1 cup dry white wine (optional)
1 pound mushrooms, sliced
1 tbsp. cornstarch
2 tbsps. water
Olive oil as needed

Directions:

1. Pound the pork chops with a spiked meat mallet until 1/4 inch thick; set aside.
2. In a large bowl, combine the bread crumbs, Parmesan cheese, parsley flakes, salt, and pepper. Press the pork into the crumbs to bread thoroughly; set aside.
3. Melt butter in a large saucepan over medium-high heat.
4. Stir in the garlic and cook until fragrant, about 30 seconds.
5. Pour in the wine and sliced mushrooms. Allow to simmer and cook until the mushrooms have softened, about 10 minutes.
6. Stir together the cornstarch and water, then add to the mushroom sauce. Simmer until the sauce has thickened, then remove from the heat and set aside.
7. Meanwhile, heat a few tbsps. of olive oil in a large, nonstick skillet over medium-high heat. Fry the pork cutlets a few at a time until golden brown and cooked through, 1 to 2 minutes per side. Serve with reserved mushroom sauce.

San Francisco Pork Chops

Ingredients:

1 tbsp. vegetable oil
4 (3/4 inch-thick) boneless pork chops, trimmed
1 clove garlic, minced
1/4 cup beef broth
1/4 cup soy sauce
2 tbsps. brown sugar
2 tsps. vegetable oil
1/4 tsp. red pepper flakes
2 tsps. cornstarch
2 tbsps. water

Directions:

1. Heat 1 tbsp. vegetable oil in a skillet over medium heat. Brown chops in hot oil, about 5 minutes per side; remove pork to a plate, reserving oil in skillet.
2. Cook and stir garlic in reserved drippings until fragrant, about 1 minute. Whisk beef broth, soy sauce, brown sugar, 2 tsps. vegetable oil, and red pepper flakes in a bowl, dissolving brown sugar. Return pork chops to skillet and pour soy sauce mixture over the chops.
3. Bring sauce to a boil, cover skillet, and reduce heat to low. Simmer chops until tender, 30 to 35 minutes, turning once halfway through cooking.
4. Transfer chops to a serving platter. Whisk cornstarch and water in a small bowl until smooth; stir into pan juices and simmer until thickened, about 5 minutes.
5. Pour sauce over chops to serve.

Pork Chops Marsala

Ingredients:

1/3 cup all-purpose flour
1/4 tsp. salt
1/4 tsp. garlic salt
3/4 tsp. garlic powder
1/2 tsp. dried oregano
1 lb. boneless pork loin chops
3 tbsps. butter
1/4 cup olive oil
2 cups sliced fresh mushrooms
1 tsp. minced garlic
1 cup Marsala wine

Directions:

1. Mix flour, salt ,garlic salt, garlic powder, and oregano together in a medium bowl.
2. Add pork chops, and toss until well coated.
3. Heat butter and olive oil in a large skillet over medium heat.
4. Place pork in skillet in a single layer, and cook, turning occasionally, until brown on both sides.
5. Add mushrooms and minced garlic; cook and stir briefly.
6. Stir in wine, scraping the skillet to loosen any brown bits.
7. Cover and simmer over medium heat until pork is tender and sauce is thickened, about 15 minutes. If sauce is too thick, adjust by stirring in a small amount of wine.

Orange BBQ Pork Chops

Ingredients:

4 lean bone-in pork chops, 3/4 inch thick
1/2 cup barbecue sauce
2 tbsp. orange marmalade
1 tsp. ground ginger
1 tsp. garlic powder

Directions:

1. Heat oven to 400 degrees F.
2. Place chops in 8-inch square baking dish sprayed with cooking spray.
3. Mix remaining ingredients until blended.
4. Pour over chops.
5. Bake 35 to 40 min. or until done (145 degrees F).
6. Remove from oven. Let stand 3 min. before serving.

Apricot Pork Chops

Ingredients:

6 pork chops
1 (1 oz.) package dry onion soup mix
10 oz. Russian-style salad dressing
1 cup apricot preserves

Directions:

1. Preheat oven to 350 degrees F (175 degrees C).
2. Place the pork chops into a casserole dish.
3. Mix onion soup mix, Russian dressing and apricot preserves together.
4. Pour mixture over chops and bake for 1 hour.

Marmalade Pork Chops

Ingredients:

5 pork chops
1/2 cup orange marmalade
1/2 cup soy sauce

Directions:

1. Preheat oven to 350 degrees F (175 degrees C).
2. Place pork chops in a 9x13 baking dish.
3. In a small bowl stir together the marmalade and soy sauce.
4. Pour over the chops.
5. Cover with foil and bake for 1 hour.

Parmesan Sage Pork Chops

Ingredients:

2 tbsps. all-purpose flour
1/4 tsp. salt
1 pinch ground black pepper
1 egg, lightly beaten
3/4 cup Italian bread crumbs
1/2 cup grated Parmesan cheese
1 1/2 tsps. rubbed sage
1/2 tsp. grated lemon zest
2 boneless pork chops
1 tbsp. olive oil
1 tbsp. butter

Directions:

1. Preheat oven to 425 degrees F (220 degrees C).
2. Lightly grease a 7x11-inch baking dish.
3. Mix flour, salt, and ground pepper in a shallow dish.
4. Combine bread crumbs, Parmesan cheese, sage, and lemon peel in a shallow dish. Gently press pork into flour mixture to coat and shake off excess flour. Dip into beaten egg, then press into bread crumbs. Gently toss between your hands so any bread crumbs that haven't stuck can fall away.
5. Place breaded pork onto a plate while breading the rest; do not stack.
6. Heat olive oil and butter in a skillet over medium heat. Brown pork chops on each side, about 4 minutes per side, then transfer to baking dish.
7. Bake in preheated oven until juices run clear and a meat thermometer inserted into the middle of pork reads 160 degrees F (71 degrees C), 10 to 15 minutes.

Stuffed Pork Chops

Pesto Stuffed Pork Chops

Ingredients:

3 tbsps. crumbled feta cheese
2 tbsps. chilled basil pesto
1 tbsp. toasted pine nuts
4 thick pork chops
1 tsp. ground black pepper
1 tsp. dried oregano
1 tsp. minced garlic
1/2 tsp. red pepper flakes
1/4 tsp. ground thyme
2 tbsps. balsamic vinegar

Directions:

1. Preheat oven to 375 degrees F
2. Mix feta cheese, basil pesto, and pine nuts in a bowl.
3. Cut a 3-inch slit in the side of each pork chop to make a pocket for stuffing.
4. Stuff pork chops with pesto filling and secure with toothpicks.
5. Mix black pepper, oregano, garlic, red pepper flakes, and thyme in a small bowl.
6. Rub both sides of each pork chop with the spice mix.
7. Place pork chops into a shallow baking dish.
8. Bake in the preheated oven until pork chops are browned and stuffing is hot, about 40 minutes.
9. Brush pork chops with balsamic vinegar and bake until vinegar forms a glaze, another 5 minutes.

Apple Stuffed Pork Chops

Ingredients:

1 tbsp. chopped onion
1/4 cup butter
3 cups fresh bread crumbs
2 cups chopped apples
1/4 cup chopped celery
2 tsps. chopped fresh parsley
1/4 tsp. salt
6 (1 1/4 inch) thick pork chops
Salt and pepper to taste
1 tbsp. vegetable oil

Directions:

1. Preheat oven to 350 degrees F (175 degrees C).
2. In a large skillet saute onion in butter or margarine until tender.
3. Remove from heat.
4. Add the bread crumbs, apples, celery, parsley and salt.
5. Mix all together.
6. Cut a large pocket in the side of each pork chop; season inside and out with salt and pepper to taste. Spoon apple mixture loosely into pockets.
7. In skillet, heat oil to medium high and brown chops on both sides.
8. Place browned chops in an ungreased 9x13 inch baking dish.
9. Cover with aluminum foil and bake in the preheated oven for 30 minutes.
10. Remove cover and bake for 30 minutes longer or until juices run clear.

Apple-Mustard Stuffed Pork Chops

Ingredients:

4 boneless pork chop s (1-1/2 lb.), 1-1/2 inches thick
1/2 cup chopped Granny Smith apples
10 buttery round crackers (like Ritz), coarsely crushed (about 1/2 cup)
1/4 cup coarsely chopped pecans
3 tbsp. Dijon Mustard, divided
2 tbsp. raisins

Directions:

1. Heat grill to medium heat.
2. Make pocket in each chop by carefully making horizontal cut in thickest side of chop, being careful to not cut all the way through to opposite side of chop.
3. Combine apples, cracker crumbs, nuts, 2 Tbsp. mustard and raisins; spoon into pockets in chops. Press cut sides together to seal pockets; secure with wooden toothpicks.
4. Grill chops 30 min. or until chops are done (145°F), turning after 15 min. and brushing with remaining mustard.
5. Remove from grill. Let stand 3 min. before removing toothpicks from chops and serving.

Apple Cranberry Stuffed Pork Chops

Ingredients:

2 tbsp. butter
1/8 yellow onion, minced
1 Granny Smith apple, peeled, cored and diced
2 stalk celery ribs, finely chopped
1/4 cup dried cranberries
1 tsp. kosher salt
5 (1 inch thick) boneless pork chops
1 cup apple juice
1 tbsp. cornstarch
2 tbsp. brown sugar
1 tsp. freshly ground black pepper

Directions:

1. Preheat oven to 350 degrees F (175 degrees C).
2. In a Dutch oven, melt 1 tbsp. butter over medium heat.
3. Cook onion
4. in butter until the onions are very so and begin to brown.
5. Remove from heat.
6. Stir in apple, celery, and dried cranberries.
7. Season with salt.
8. Lay each chop flat on cutting board, and with a sharp knife held parallel to the board, cut a pocket into the pork, leaving three sides intact.
9. Stuff each chop with apple-cranberry mixture.
10. Melt remaining butter in the Dutch oven over medium heat. Pan-fry chops in butter for two minutes on each side.
11. Cover, and bake in preheated oven for 45 minutes.
12. Transfer chops from pan to a plate, and cover with foil.
13. Place the Dutch oven back on the stovetop over medium heat.
14. In a small bowl or measuring cup, stir together apple juice, cornstarch, and brown sugar.
15. Pour into Dutch oven.
16. Reduce liquid volume by half, stirring frequently.
17. Season to taste with black pepper.
18. Serve this apple glaze over pork chops.

Gouda and Spinach Stuffed Pork Chops

Ingredients:

4 (6 oz.) thick cut pork chops
8 slices smoked Gouda cheese
1/2 pound fresh spinach, torn into bite-size pieces
3 tbsps. horseradish mustard
1 cup breadcrumbs
Creole-style seasoning to taste

Directions:

1. Preheat the oven to 400 degrees F.
2. Coat a baking dish with cooking spray.
3. Lay each pork chop flat on a cutting board, and with a sharp knife held parallel to the board, cut a pocket into the pork, leaving three sides intact.
4. Stuff each chop with spinach and cheese.
5. Place bread crumbs in a shallow dish.
6. Coat each pork chop with a thin layer of horseradish, and then roll in crumbs.
7. Arrange pork chops in prepared baking dish.
8. Sprinkle with Creole seasoning to taste.
9. Bake for 45 minutes, or until brown and crispy.

Bacon-Stuffed Chops with Creamy Balsamic Sauce

Ingredients:

2 (6 oz.) thick-cut pork chops

Stuffing Ingredients:

1 tbsp. butter
2 tbsps. bacon bits
2 tsps. Worcestershire sauce
2 tsps. chopped onion
1/2 tsp. prepared yellow mustard
1/2 clove garlic, minced
8 toothpicks, or as needed

Sauce Ingredients:

2 tbsps. butter
1 clove garlic, minced
1/2 cup balsamic vinegar
1/4 cup Worcestershire sauce
1 tsp. prepared yellow mustard
2 cups sour cream

Directions:

1. Preheat oven to 350 degrees F (175 degrees C).
2. Lay a pork chop flat on your work surface. Use the tip of a sharp boning or paring knife to create a pocket by making a slit in the side; repeat with remaining pork chops.
3. Melt 1 tbsp. butter in a skillet over medium heat; add bacon bits, 2 tsps. Worcestershire sauce, onion, 1/2 tsp. mustard, and 1/2 clove garlicup Cook and stir until onion is soft and translucent, about 5 minutes.
4. Allow stuffing to cool, 5 to 10 minutes. Stuff into pork chops and secure with 2 crossed toothpicks.
5. Heat 2 tbsps. of butter in a large skillet over medium heat. Brown pork chops, about 2 minutes per side. Transfer to a baking dish, reserving drippings in skillet.
6. Cover baking dish with aluminum foil.
7. Bake in the preheated oven until pork chops are no longer pink in the center, about 30 minutes. An instant-read thermometer inserted into the center should read 145 degrees F (63 degrees C).
8. Heat reserved drippings in the skillet over medium heat.
9. Add 1 clove garlic, balsamic vinegar, 1/4 cup Worcestershire sauce, and 1 tsp. mustard; simmer until reduced, about 5 minutes.
10. Stir in sour cream. Coat pork chops with sauce.

Pork Chops With Dates And Manchego Stuffing

Ingredients:

6 double-thick bone-in rib pork chops, about 12 oz. each
2 cups apple cider vinegar
1 cup light brown sugar, packed
1/2 cup sea salt
1 tbsp. dry mustard
1 tbsp. black peppercorns
1/2 gallon ice water
Chorizo Stuffing:
2 tbsps. unsalted butter
1 pound smoked Spanish chorizo, diced
2 medium celery, finely chopped
1/3 cup dates, pitted and finely chopped
2 tbsps. shallot, finely chopped
1 tbsp. fresh parsley, minced
2 tsps. fresh sage, minced
1/2 tsp. smoked paprika
1 cup (4 oz.) Manchego cheese, or sharp Cheddar cheese, shredded
Sea salt
Freshly ground black pepper, to taste

Brine Directions:

1. Bring vinegar, brown sugar, salt, mustard, and peppercorns to a simmer over medium heat, stirring to dissolve salt. Do not inhale fumes. Transfer to large, deep food-safe container. Let cool until tepid.
2. Stir in iced water. Submerge chops in brine. Refrigerate for 3 hours (no longer).

Stuffing Directions:

1. Melt butter in a large skillet over medium heat.
2. Add chorizo and cook, stirring occasionally, until lightly browned, about 5 minutes.
3. Add celery, dates, and shallot, and cook, stirring often, until celery is tender, about 5 minutes.
4. Stir in parsley, sage, and paprika. Transfer to a bowl and let cool completely.
5. Stir in cheese and season with salt and pepper.
6. Remove chops from brine, rinse under cold water, and blot dry with paper towels.
7. Cut a horizontal pocket in each chop to the bone using a sharp knife. Spoon equal amounts of stuffing into each chop, and close each opening shut with wooden toothpicks. Do not overstuff the chops.
8. Prepare a medium fire in an outdoor grill.

9. For a gas grill, preheat to about 400 degrees F. For a charcoal grill, let the coals burn until covered with white ash and you can hold your hand about an inch above the cooking grate for 3 seconds.
10. Brush cooking grates clean.
11. Grill pork, with the lid closed as much as possible, turning occasionally, until an instant-read thermometer inserted horizontally into the center of a chop reads 145°F, about 15 minutes.
12. Remove from the grill and let stand for 3 to 5 minutes.
13. Remove toothpicks and serve.

Mushroom Savory Stuffed Pork Chops

Ingredients:

4 pork chops
Salt and pepper
2 tbsp. butter
1/2 cup chopped onion
1 cup chopped mushrooms
1/4 tsp. dried sage
1/4 tsp. salt
1/4 tsp. pepper
1 cup bread crumbs
2 tsps. vegetable broth

Directions:

1. Preheat oven 350 degrees F.
2. Trim fat from chops.
3. Cut a 2 inch pocket in each pork chop.
4. Sprinkle inside of each pocket with salt and pepper.
5. Set aside.
6. Melt butter in a large skillet over medium heat.
7. Add onion and mushrooms.
8. Sauté until tender.
9. Remove from heat.
10. Stir in sage, salt, pepper and bread crumbs.
11. Add enough broth to moisten and hold stuffing together.
12. Spoon stuffing in to pockets.
13. Secure pockets with kitchen twine or toothpicks.
14. Place chops in baking dish.
15. Add remaining broth.
16. Cover and bake for 30 minutes.
17. Remove cover and bake for 20 minutes or until tender.
18. Serve and enjoy!

Blue Cheese, Bacon and Chive Stuffed Pork Chops

Ingredients:

2 boneless pork loin chops, butterflied
4 oz. crumbled blue cheese
2 slices bacon, cooked and crumbled
2 tbsps. chopped fresh chives
Garlic salt to taste
Ground black pepper to taste
Chopped fresh parsley for garnish

Directions:

1. Preheat the oven to 325 degrees F (165 degrees C).
2. Grease a shallow baking dish.
3. In a small bowl, mix together the blue cheese, bacon and chives. Divide into halves, and pack each half into a loose ball.
4. Place each one into a pocket of a butterflied pork chop, close, and secure with toothpicks.
5. Season each chop with garlic salt and pepper. Keep in mind that the blue cheese will be salty.
6. Place in the prepared baking dish.
7. Bake for 20 minutes in the preheated oven, or it may take longer if your chops are thicker.
8. Cook until the stuffing is hot, and chops are to your desired degree of doneness. Garnish with fresh parsley and serve.

Couscous Stuffed Pork Chops

Ingredients:

1 1/2 cups chicken broth, divided
5 tbsps. butter, divided
3/4 cup dry couscous
1 small onion, finely chopped
2 cloves garlic, minced
1/2 cup currants
1/2 cup pine nuts
1/8 tsp. ground cinnamon
Salt and freshly ground black pepper
6 boneless pork loin chops, butterflied
1/2 cup orange marmalade

Directions:

1. Combine 1 1/4 cups chicken broth and 2 tbsps. butter in a saucepan. (Set aside remaining chicken broth.) Bring to a boil over medium heat.
2. Stir in couscous, cover, and remove from heat. Let stand until liquid is absorbed, about 10 minutes. Fluff couscous with a fork.
3. In a frying pan over medium heat, melt the remaining 3 tbsps. butter.
4. Cook onion and garlic in butter until tender, about 5 minutes.
5. Remove pan from heat, and stir in currants, pine nuts, cooked couscous, and cinnamon.
6. Season to taste with salt and pepper.
7. Toss the mixture with as much of the reserved chicken stock as needed to hold together slightly.
8. Preheat the oven to 350 degrees F (180 degrees C).
9. Lightly oil a roasting pan or large baking dish.
10. Reserve about 1/3 cup stuffing to sprinkle over the chops. Stuff each chop generously with stuffing, and insert toothpicks to keep the chops closed.
11. Place the pork chops in an oiled roasting pan just large enough to hold them comfortably, and coat each generously with the marmalade.
12. Sprinkle with the reserved stuffing, and press stuffing lightly into the marmalade so that it will stick to the chops.
13. Bake in the preheated oven until the chops are browned on the outside, but just slightly pink in the center, about 40 to 45 minutes. Transfer the pork chops to warmed individual plates, remove the toothpicks, and serve hot.

Buttery Corn Stuffed Pork Chops

Ingredients:

1 1/2 cups dry bread crumbs
2 tbsps. butter
1 egg, beaten
2 cups whole kernel corn
4 pork chops butterfly cut
1 (10.75 oz.) can condensed cream of mushroom soup

Directions:

1. Preheat oven to 350 degrees F (175 degrees C).
2. In bowl, combine bread crumbs, butter, egg, and corn.
3. Mix until it is a stiff stuffing.
4. Cut parallel into each chop to create a pocket. Stuff each pork chop with stuffing mix.
5. Place chops in a cooking dish and then pour mushroom soup over top.
6. Bake for about 45 minutes or until chops are cooked all the way through.

Cream Corn Pork Chops

Ingredients:

2 (15 oz.) cans creamed corn
4 pork chops
1/4 tbsp. garlic powder
Salt and pepper to taste

Directions:

1. Preheat oven to 350 degrees F (175 degrees C).
2. Spread corn in the bottom of a 9x13 inch baking dish, then place pork chops on top of corn.
3. Press the chops down into the corn.
4. Cover dish with aluminum foil and bake in the preheated oven for 1 1/2 to 2 hours, or until internal temperature of pork has reached 145 degrees F (63 degrees C).

Ham and Cheese Stuffed Pork Chop

Ingredients:

4 (4 oz. each) boneless pork loin chops
4 slices Ham, any variety
4 slices Swiss cheese
1/2 cup baby spinach leaves
1 tbsp. dried sage leaves, crushed
1 tsp. olive oil

Directions:

1. Make a 2-inch long cut in the side of each chop to form pocket. Top each ham slice with 1 Singles and 1/4 of the spinach; roll up. Stuff 1 ham roll in pocket in each chop; press edges of pocket together to seal.
2. Sprinkle both sides of chops evenly with sage.
3. Heat oil in large skillet on medium-high heat.
4. Add chops; cook 8 to 10 min. on each side or until cooked through and golden brown on both sides.

Bacon Wrapped Pork Chops

Ingredients:

6 (1 inch thick) boneless pork chops
6 tbsps. process cheese sauce
12 slices bacon

Directions:

1. Preheat the oven to 350 degrees F (175 degrees C). Fry the bacon in a skillet over medium heat until cooked through but still flexible.
2. Wrap two slices of bacon around each pork chop and top with a tbsp. of cheese sauce.
3. Place the pork chops in a baking dish.
4. Bake for 1 hour in the preheated oven.

Cheesy Rice Stuffed Pork Chops

Ingredients:

3 tbsps. unsalted butter divided
1 small yellow onion finely chopped
1 cup cooked white rice (Jasmine)
3/4 cup chicken broth divided
1/2 cup mozzarella cheese
1/2 cup ricotta cheese
2 tbsps. parmesan cheese freshly grated
Kosher salt and freshly cracked pepper to taste
1 tbsp. fresh thyme chopped, plus more for garnish
4 boneless center cut pork chops

Directions:

1. Melt 2 tbsps. of the butter In a medium nonstick pan over medium heat.
2. Add onion and a pinch of salt; saute until softened, about 5 to 7 minutes.
3. While the onions are cooking, cut a deep horizontal pocket in each chop with a knife, making sure not to cut all the way through.
4. Season with salt and pepper to taste; set aside.
5. When the onions are soft, turn off the heat; stir in rice, ¼ cup of the chicken broth, cheeses and thyme.
6. Mix well.
7. Spoon the rice mixture into the pockets of each pork chop dividing evenly; secure openings with toothpicks. If you have any of the rice mixture left over, reserve for serving with the pork chops.
8. Melt the remaining tbsp. of the butter in a cast iron or stainless steel pan.
9. Add stuffed pork chops; cook until browned, turning only once, about 2 to 3 minutes on each side.
10. Add remaining broth; cover, reduce heat to medium and cook until chops are cooked through, about 10 to 15 minutes, depending on thickness.
11. Remove the toothpicks and serve garnished with thyme sprigs, extra stuffing mixture and pan drippings on the side.

Pork Chops With Sauerkraut Stuffing

Ingredients:

5 cup herb seasoned croutons
2 cup sauerkraut
3 tbsp. brown sugar, firmly packed
1 cup thinly sliced pared apples
2 tbsp. shortening
6 pork loin chops, 3/4 inch thick
Salt and pepper to taste

Directions:

1. Pour croutons into a mixing bowl.
2. Add sauerkraut, brown sugar, and apples.
3. Stir until combined. Set aside, heat shortening in a fry pan. Brown pork chops on both sides; add salt and pepper to taste.
4. Place in bottom of a greased shallow 2 quart rectangular baking dish. Spoon stuffing evenly over chops.
5. Cover tightly with aluminum foil.
6. Bake at 350 degrees for 1 hour and 15 minutes.

Pizza Stuffed Pork Chops

Ingredients:

6 double rib pork chops
1 recipe Stove Top stuffing
1 (5 1/2 oz.) can pizza sauce
1 (8 oz.) can tomato sauce
3 slices sharp cheese

Directions:

1. Cut pocket in pork chops and trim off any excess fat. Stuff with Stove Top dressing and place in shallow pan.
2. Place one layer deep.
3. Cover with pizza sauce, then tomato sauce.
4. Cover with foil.
5. Bake at 350 degrees for 1 1/2 hours. Top with cheese.

Cranberry Rice Stuffed Pork Chops

Ingredients:

1 package whole grain brown instant rice
1/2 cup whole cranberry sauce
1/2 cup barbecue sauce
1 tbsp. orange zest
2 tbsp. orange juice
1/2 tsp. minced garlic
4 (5-oz) boneless pork chops, (about 3/4 inch thick)
1/4 tsp. each salt and pepper

Directions:

1. Cook rice according to directions on the pack and preheat oven to 375 degrees F
2. Mix together cranberry sauce, barbecue sauce, orange zest, orange juice, and garlic in a small bowl. Split into two halves and set one half aside.
3. Gently stir in 1 cup of warm rice into one half of the mixture. Reserve remaining rice for another use.
4. Cut a horizontal slit through the thickest portion of each pork chop to form a pocket. Stuff 1/4 to 1/3 cup of the rice mixture into each pocket. (Wooden picks help secure the pork chops if needed).
5. Brush the chops with half of the remaining barbecue sauce mixture and bake for 30-40 minutes. Then brush the remaining barbecue sauce mixture onto chops.

Cranberry and Apple Stuffed Pork Chops

Ingredients:

1 tbsp. olive oil
1/2 onion, chopped
1 large Granny Smith apple, peeled, cored and diced
2 tbsps. balsamic vinegar
1/2 cup dried cranberries
Salt and pepper to taste
2 (6 oz.) boneless pork chops
1 tbsp. olive oil

Directions:

1. Heat 1 tbsp. olive oil in a skillet over medium heat.
2. Stir in the onion and apple; cook and stir for 5 minutes.
3. Stir in the cranberries and balsamic vinegar, and continue cooking until the apple and onions have softened, about 5 minutes more.
4. Season to taste with salt and pepper, then scrape the mixture onto a plate, and refrigerate until cold.
5. Preheat oven to 350 degrees F (175 degrees C).
6. Lightly grease a small baking dish.
7. Cut a large pocket into the pork chops using a sharp, thin bladed knife. Stuff the cooled apple mixture into the pork chops, and secure with toothpicks if needed.
8. Heat the remaining 1 tbsp. olive oil in a large skillet over medium-high heat.
9. Season the pork chops with salt and pepper to taste, and place into the hot skillet.
10. Cook on each side until browned, about 3 minutes, then transfer to a baking dish. Top with the remaining apple mixture, and cover the baking dish with aluminum foil.
11. Bake in preheated oven until the pork is no longer pink in the center, about 40 minutes depending on the thickness of the pork chops. Uncover, and bake about 10 minutes longer until the apple mixture has browned around the edges.

Swiss Mushroom Stuffed Pork Chops

Ingredients:

2 (3/4 inch thick) bone-in pork chops
1 (4 oz.) package sliced fresh mushrooms
4 oz. diced Swiss cheese
1 tbsp. chopped fresh parsley
1 tsp. garlic powder
1/4 tsp. ground black pepper
1/4 tsp. salt
2 eggs
3/4 cup bread crumbs
2 tbsps. vegetable oil
1/2 cup white Zinfandel wine, or as needed

Directions:

1. Lay pork chops flat onto your work surface. Use the tip of a sharp boning or paring knife to cut a pocket in each pork chop making a 2 inch slit in the side.
2. Mix mushrooms, Swiss cheese, parsley, garlic powder, black pepper, and salt in a bowl; stuff pork chops with mushroom mixture. Secure the open side with a toothpick.
3. Whisk eggs in a bowl; pour bread crumbs into a separate bowl. Dip the stuffed pork chops into the beaten egg; press pork chops into bread crumbs until completely coated.
4. Heat oil in a skillet over medium heat; place pork chops, pocket side-down, into the hot oil.
5. Cook until outside of pork chops is browned, 2 to 3 minutes per side.
6. Pour in enough wine to come halfway up pork chops.
7. Reduce heat to low, cover skillet, and simmer until pork chops are tender, about 2 hours. Check wine level occasionally and add more as needed. An instant-read thermometer inserted into the center should read 145 degrees F (63 degrees C).

Grilled Pork Chops

Maryland Pork Chops

Ingredients:

1/2 cup vegetable oil
1/2 cup apple cider vinegar
1 tbsp. seafood seasoning (such as Old Bay)
2 cloves minced garlic
1 tbsp. chopped fresh basil
1 lime, juiced
Cracked black pepper to taste
8 boneless pork chops, 1/2 inch thick

Directions:

1. Whisk together the vegetable oil, apple cider vinegar, seafood seasoning, minced garlic, basil, lime juice, and black pepper in a bowl, and pour into a resealable plastic bag.
2. Add the pork chops, coat with the marinade, squeeze out excess air, and seal the bag. Marinate in the refrigerator for 4 to 6 hours, flipping periodically.
3. Preheat an outdoor grill for medium-high heat, and lightly oil the grate.
4. Remove the pork chops from the bags. Discard excess marinade.
5. Grill until the pork is no longer pink in the center, 5 to 7 minutes per side. An instant-read thermometer inserted into the center should read 145 degrees F (63 degrees C).

Honey Grilled Pork Chops

Ingredients:

4 1" thick boneless pork chops
1/4 cup honey
2 tbsp. Dijon mustard
1 tbsp. orange juice
1/4 tsp dried tarragon
1 tsp. cider vinegar
1/2 tsp Worcester sauce
1/8 tsp garlic powder

Directions:

1. Preheat grill.
2. Brush rack with vegetable oil.
3. Trim excess fat from chops.
4. Score outer edge of meat at 1" intervals.
5. Blend honey, mustard, orange juice, tarragon, vinegar, Worcestershire sauce and garlic powder in a small bowl.
6. Place chops on the grill about 4 inches from heat.
7. Brush with honey mixture.
8. Grill for 8 minutes, brushing every 2 minutes with honey mixture.
9. Turn chops over.
10. Grill for 8 minutes longer or until cooked through, basting every 2 minutes with honey mixture.
11. Serve and enjoy!

Adobo Pork Chops

Ingredients:

6 boneless pork loin chops 3/4-inch thick
2 tbsp. packed light brown sugar
2 tbsp. extra virgin olive oil
2 tbsp. low-sugar orange juice
2 tsp. dried cilantro
1 tbsp. red-wine vinegar
2 tbsp. chili powder
1 tsp. ground cumin
1/2 tsp. dried oregano
1/2 tsp. salt
1/4 tsp. cayenne pepper
1/4 tsp. ground cinnamon
3 tsp. minced garlic

Directions:

1. Trim fat from chops.
2. Place chops in a resealable bag, place bag in a shallow dish.
3. In a large bowl, combine brown sugar, oil, orange juice, cilantro, vinegar, chili powder, cumin, oregano, salt, cayenne pepper, cinnamon, and garlicup Pour marinade over chops. Marinate in a ziploc bag for 2 hours in refrigerator, turning bag occasionally.
4. Drain chops, discard marinade.
5. Start grill. When grill is hot, place chops directly over heat.
6. Grill about 12 minutes. Turn over.
7. Grill another 12-15 minutes or until juices run clear.

Hawaiian Pork Chops

Ingredients:

1/4 pineapple, peeled, cored, cut into chunks
2 jalapeño chilies, sliced
1 garlic clove, chopped
1/4 cup cilantro leaves with tender stems
2 tbsps. soy sauce
1 tbsp. fish sauce
4 pork chops

Directions:

1. Mix pineapple with chilies, garlic, cilantro, soy sauce, and fish sauce.
2. Before marinating, set some marinade aside to use as a dipping sauce.
3. Pour the rest over the pork chops.
4. Cover; chill at least 6 hours and up to 1 day.
5. Remove pork from marinade.
6. Grill or broil pork chops until done.
7. Serve and enjoy!

Carolina Gold Grilled Pork Chops

Ingredients:

3 tbsps. dry mustard
2 tbsps. kosher salt
2 tbsps. packed brown sugar
2 tsps. black pepper
2 tsps. paprika
1/4 tsp. cayenne pepper

Directions:

1. Mix together all the ingredients.
2. Sprinkle generously over pork or chicken. Store any remaining in an air tight container.

Pineapple Teriyaki Pork Chops

Ingredients:

4 boneless pork chops
1/4 cup teriyaki sauce
1 tbsp. sugar
2 tbsps. pineapple juice

Directions:

1. Combine teriyaki, sugar and pineapple juice in a large resealable bag.
2. Mix well.
3. Add pork chops. Put in refrigerator and let marinare for 4-6 hours, turning occasionally.
4. Remove chops from mixture; cook on hot grill for 7 minutes on each side or until chops are done.

Asian Style Pork Chops

Ingredients:

1/2 cup orange juice
2 tbsps. soy sauce
2 tbsps. minced fresh ginger root
2 tbsps. grated orange zest
1 tsp. minced garlic
1 tsp. garlic chili paste
1/2 tsp. salt
6 pork loin chops, 1/2 inch thick

Directions:

1. In a shallow container, mix together orange juice, soy sauce, ginger, orange zest, garlic, chili paste, and salt.
2. Add pork chops, and turn to coat evenly.
3. Cover, and refrigerate for at least 2 hours, or overnight.
4. Turn the pork chops in the marinade occasionally.
5. Preheat grill for high heat, and lightly oil grate.
6. Grill pork chops for 5 to 6 minutes per side, or until done.
7. Serve and enjoy!

Cuban Pork Chops

Ingredients:

1 tbsp. Dijon mustard
1 tbsp. lime juice
2 tbsps. chopped fresh cilantro
Optional ingredients:
Mayonnaise
Additional Dijon mustard
Dill pickles, thinly sliced

Directions:

1. Mix mustard, lime juice and adobo seasoning in a small bowl.
2. Lightly pound pork chops with a meat mallet to 1/2-in. thickness.
3. Spread both sides with mustard mixture.
4. Refrigerate, covered, 3-4 hours.
5. Grill pork, covered, over medium heat 3 minutes.
6. Turn pork and top with ham; grill 2 minutes longer.
7. Top with cheese and cilantro.
8. Close the grill lid, for about 30-60 seconds to let the cheese melt.
9. Let stand 5 minutes before serving.
10. Serve with mayonnaise, mustard and pickles.

Pork Chops With Cranberry Cucumber Relish

Ingredients:

4 bone-in pork chops, about 1" thick
1/2 cup hawaiian marinade
2 tbsps. Hawaiian Marinade
1 large red bell pepper, diced
1 medium cucumber, peeled, seeded and diced
1/2 cup chopped dried cranberries
1/4 cup diced red onion

Directions:

1. Place pork chops in large resealable plastic bag or glass dish.
2. Add 1/2 cup of the marinade; turn to coat well. Refrigerate 30 minutes.
3. Meanwhile, mix bell pepper, cucumber, cranberries, onion and remaining 2 tbsps. marinade in large bowl; toss to coat. Set aside.
4. Remove pork chops from marinade. Discard any remaining marinade.
5. Grill over medium heat 6 to 7 minutes per side or until desired doneness, brushing with additional marinade if desired. Serve pork chops with relish.

Basil-Garlic Grilled Pork Chops

Ingredients:

4 (8 oz.) pork chops
1 lime, juiced
4 cloves garlic, minced
1/4 cup chopped fresh basil
Salt and black pepper to taste

Directions:

1. Toss the pork chops with the lime juice in a bowl until evenly covered.
2. Toss with garlic and basil.
3. Season the chops to taste with salt and pepper. Set aside to marinate for 30 minutes.
4. Preheat an outdoor grill for medium heat, and lightly oil the grate.
5. Cook the pork chops on the preheated grill until no longer pink in the center, 5 to 10 minutes per side. An instant-read thermometer inserted into the center should read 145 degrees F (63 degrees C).

Dijon Grilled Pork Chops

Ingredients:

6 tbsps. Dijon mustard
6 tbsps. brown sugar
3 tbsps. unsweetened apple juice
3 tbsps. Worcestershire sauce
4 (8 oz.) bone-in pork loin chops

Directions:

1. Mix mustard, brown sugar, apple juice, and Worcestershire sauce together in a bowl until marinade is smooth.
2. Pour 2/3 the marinade into a large resealable plastic bag.
3. Add pork chops, coat with marinade, squeeze out excess air, and seal the bag. Marinate in the refrigerator for 8 hours to overnight.
4. Cover bowl with remaining marinade with plastic wrap and refrigerate.
5. Remove pork chops from marinade and discard bag and marinade.
6. Preheat grill for medium heat and lightly oil the grate.
7. Cook the pork chops on the preheated grill, basting with reserved marinade, until no longer pink in the center, 4 to 5 minutes per side.
8. An instant-read thermometer inserted into the center should read 145 degrees F (63 degrees C).
9. Let pork chops stand for 5 minutes before serving.

Grilled Brown Sugar Pork Chops

Ingredients:

1/2 cup brown sugar, firmly packed
1/2 cup apple juice
4 tbsps. vegetable oil
1 tbsp. soy sauce
1/2 tsp. ground ginger
Salt and pepper to taste
2 tsps. cornstarch
1/2 cup water
6 boneless pork chops

Directions:

1. Preheat an outdoor grill for high heat.
2. In a small saucepan, combine brown sugar, apple juice, oil, soy sauce, ginger, salt , and pepper.
3. Bring to boil.
4. Combine water and cornstarch in small bowl, and whisk into brown sugar mixture.
5. Stir until thick.
6. Brush grate lightly with oil before placing pork chops on the grill.
7. Cook over hot coals for 10 to 12 minutes, turning once. Brush with sauce just before removing chops from grill.
8. Serve with remaining sauce.

Pizza Pork Chops

Ingredients:

5 boneless pork chops
1 pinch salt and ground black pepper to taste
5 slices tomato (
1/2-inch thick)
1/4 cup chopped fresh basil
1 tbsp. chopped fresh oregano
2 cloves garlic, minced
2 tbsps. olive oil
5 slices mozzarella cheese

Directions:

1. Preheat an outdoor grill for medium heat.
2. Season the pork chops with salt and black pepper and arrange in the bottom of a disposable aluminum pan; top each with a tomato slice. Divide the basil, oregano, and garlic between the pork chops; drizzle with the olive oil.
3. Cover the pan with aluminum foil.
4. Cook on the preheated grill until the pork is no longer pink in the center, about 25 minutes. An instant-read thermometer inserted into the center should read 145 degrees F (63 degrees C).
5. Remove the pan from the grill; top each pork chop with a slice of mozzarella cheese, replace the aluminum foil over the pan, and wait until the cheese melts, 3 to 5 minutes, before serving.

Grilled Mongolian Pork Chops

Ingredients:

1/2 cup hoisin sauce
4 cloves garlic, minced
1 1/2 tbsps. soy sauce
1 tbsp. grated fresh ginger
1 tbsp. red wine vinegar
1 tbsp. rice vinegar
1 tbsp. sherry vinegar
2 tsps. sesame oil
2 tsps. white sugar
1 1/2 tsps. hot sauce
1/2 tsp. ground white pepper
1/2 tsp. freshly ground black pepper
2 (10 oz.) thick bone-in center cut pork chops
1/4 cup red wine vinegar
3 tbsps. white sugar
2 tbsps. hot mustard powder or Chinese style
1 egg yolk
1/3 cup creme fraiche
1 tsp. Dijon mustard
1/4 tsp. ground turmeric
Cayenne pepper to taste

Directions:

1. Combine hoisin sauce, garlic, soy sauce, ginger, 1 tbsp. red wine vinegar, rice vinegar, sherry vinegar, sesame oil, 2 tsps. sugar, hot sauce, white pepper, and black pepper in a large bowl.
2. Whisk thoroughly and set aside.
3. Place pork chops in a resealable freezer bag; pour slightly more than 1/2 the marinade into freezer bag over pork chops. Seal bag and refrigerate for 6 to 8 hours. Reserve remaining marinade.
4. Combine 1/4 cup red wine vinegar, 3 tbsps. sugar, 2 tbsps. hot mustard powder, and egg yolk in a small saucepan over medium-low heat.
5. Whisk until slightly thickened, about 5 minutes; remove from heat.
6. Stir in creme fraiche, Dijon mustard, turmeric, and cayenne pepper. Refrigerate until needed.
7. Remove pork chops from marinade and pat dry using paper towel.
8. Preheat an outdoor grill for high heat, and lightly oil the grate.
9. Cook pork chops on the preheated grill until browned grill marks appear, about 4 minutes per side.
10. Move pork chops from directly above heat source. Continue cooking over indirect medium heat, brushing the remaining marinade on each side, until no longer pink inside, about 25 minutes.
11. Serve pork chops topped with mustard sauce.

Grilled Italian Pork Chops

Ingredients:

4 (3/4 inch thick) pork chops
Salt and ground black pepper to taste
4 slices ham4 slices tomato
4 slices mozzarella cheese
Chopped fresh oregano to taste
Paprika to taste

Directions:

1. Preheat an outdoor grill for medium heat, and lightly oil the grate.
2. Sprinkle pork chops with salt and black pepper, and grill until the chops are browned, show good grill marks, and are no longer pink in the middle, 5 to 8 minutes per side.
3. An instant-read meat thermometer inserted into the center of a chop should read at least 145 degrees F (63 degrees C).
4. Place ham, tomato, and mozzarella cheese slices on each pork chop, and sprinkle with oregano and paprika; cook until the cheese has melted, about 2 more minutes. Let stand for 5 minutes before serving.

Molasses Brined Pork Chops

Ingredients:

1/2 cup kosher salt
1/2 cup molasses
4 whole cloves
1 cup boiling water
7 cups cold water
4 (2 1/4 inch thick) center cut, bone-in pork chops
1/2 tsp. vegetable oil

Directions:

1. Combine salt, molasses, cloves, and boiling water in a large container.
2. Stir until molasses and salt are dissolved; let cool to room temperature.
3. Pour cold water into molasses mixture; stir to combine.
4. Completely submerge pork chops in molasses mixture.
5. Cover container and refrigerate for 6 hours.
6. Remove pork chops from brine and pat dry with paper towels.
7. Lightly oil each chop.
8. Preheat an outdoor grill for medium-high heat and lightly oil the grate.
9. Place pork chops on the hottest part of the grill.
10. Cook each side until browned, 2 to 3 minutes.
11. Transfer to a medium-high area of the grill and cook pork until it is slightly pink in the center, 6 to 8 minutes per side.
12. An instant-read thermometer inserted into the center of the chop should read 145 degrees F (63 degrees C).

Pork Chops with Balsamic Caramelized Pears

Ingredients:

1/2 quart water
5 tbsp. kosher salt
2 tbsp. white sugar
6 pork loin chops, 1/2 inch thick
1/2 cup olive oil
4 clove garlic, minced
1 tbsp. fresh rosemary, minced
1/2 cup balsamic vinegar
1 tbsp. butter
1 tbsp. olive oil
2 Vidalia onions, each cut into 8 wedges
2 pears, cored and each cut into 8 wedges
1 tsp. salt

Directions:

1. In a large bowl, stir together the water, kosher salt, and sugar.
2. Add pork
3. chops to this brine, and let them soak for no more than one hour.
4. Drain
5. and discard the brine. Pat pork chops dry with paper towels.
6. In a shallow dish, stir together the olive oil, garlic, and rosemary.
7. Place pork chops in the dish, and turn to coat.
8. Cover, and marinate in the
9. refrigerator for at least 1 or 2 hours.
10. Pour the balsamic vinegar into a small saucepan.
11. Bring to a boil, and cook until reduced by 1/2, about 10 minutes. When the vinegar cools, it should be the consistency of syrup.
12. Melt butter with olive oil in a large skillet over medium-high heat.
13. Add the onions and pears, and quickly brown being careful to keep the wedges intact.
14. Once the onions and pears are browned, reduce heat to low, and cook for about 7 minutes, or until tender.
15. Stir in the reduced vinegar and salt. The recipe can be prepared up to this point several hours before grilling.
16. Preheat the grill for medium-high heat.
17. Warm pears on a cool section of the grill (in the skillet), while placing the pork chops over the hot part.
18. Cook for about 3 minutes per side, or to desired doneness.
19. Remove to a serving plate, cover with aluminum foil and let rest for a few minutes. Uncover, top with the pear onion sauce, and serve.

Mediterranean Grilled Pork Chops

Ingredients:

2 tsps. dried sage, crumbled
2 tsps. dried rosemary leaves, crumbled
1 tsp. dried thyme
1 tsp. fennel seed, crushed
1/2 tsp. white sugar
1 bay leaf, crumbled
1 1/2 tsps. salt
4 bone-in pork rib chops
1/2-inch thick
1/3 cup extra-virgin olive oil

Directions:

1. In a bowl, mix together the sage, rosemary, thyme, fennel seed, sugar, bay leaf, and salt until thoroughly combined.
2. Rub both sides of the pork chops with the herb mixture, and coat them with olive oil.
3. Refrigerate several hours or overnight.
4. Preheat an outdoor grill for medium heat, and lightly oil the grate.
5. Grill the chops until they are browned, show good grill marks, and the meat is no longer pink inside, about 4 minutes per side.

Pomegranate Marinated Pork Chops

Ingredients:

1/4 cup olive oil
1 tbsp. pomegranate-infused red wine vinegar
3 sprigs fresh rosemary, leaves stripped and finely chopped
1 clove garlic, sliced
1/8 tsp. cracked black pepper
6 (1/2 inch thick) boneless pork chops
Salt

Directions:

1. Whisk olive oil, vinegar, rosemary, garlic, and black pepper together in a large glass or ceramic bowl.
2. Add the pork chops and toss to evenly coat.
3. Cover the bowl with plastic wrap and marinate in the refrigerator for 8 hours or overnight.
4. Preheat an outdoor grill for medium-high heat and lightly oil the grate.
5. Remove pork chops from marinade, discard marinade, and season pork chops with salt.
6. Cook the pork chops on the preheated grill until no longer pink in the center, 7 to 10 minutes per side.
7. An instant-read thermometer inserted into the center should read 145 degrees F (63 degrees C). Let chops rest for 3 to 5 minutes before serving.

Cherry Chutney Grilled Chops

Ingredients:

2 cups cider vinegar
2 tsps. salt
1 tsp. garlic powder
1 tsp. dried basil
1/2 tsp. crushed red pepper flakes
8 bone-in pork chops
1 (12 oz.) package frozen black cherries, thawed
1 cup water
1/2 cup white sugar
2 tbsps. chopped fresh mint

Directions:

1. Whisk together the vinegar, salt, garlic powder, basil, and red pepper flakes in a large glass or ceramic bowl.
2. Add the pork chops and toss to coat.
3. Cover the bowl with plastic wrap; marinate in the refrigerator 6 hours to overnight.
4. Preheat an outdoor grill for medium-high heat; lightly oil the grate.
5. While the grill heats, combine the cherries, water, and sugar in a saucepan over medium-low heat.
6. Cook, stirring occasionally, until the sugar dissolves completely, 5 to 10 minutes.
7. Remove the pork chops from the marinade and shake off excess moisture.
8. Discard the remaining marinade.
9. Cook the pork chops on the preheated grill until no longer pink in the center, 8 to 10 minutes per side. An instant-read thermometer inserted into the center should read 160 degrees F (70 degrees C).
10. Drizzle the chutney over the pork chops; garnish with the mint.

Smoky Grilled Pork Chops

Ingredients:

1 tbsp. seasoned salt
1 tsp. ground black pepper
1 tbsp. garlic powder
1 tbsp. onion powder
1 tbsp. ground paprika
2 tsps. Worcestershire sauce
1 tsp. liquid smoke flavoring
4 bone-in pork chops

Directions:

1. Preheat an outdoor grill for medium heat, and lightly oil the grate.
2. In a bowl, mix together the seasoned salt, black pepper, garlic powder, onion powder, paprika, Worcestershire sauce, and smoke flavoring until thoroughly combined.
3. Rinse pork chops, and sprinkle the wet chops on both sides with the spice mixture. With your hands, massage the spice rub into the meat; allow to stand for 10 minutes.
4. Grill the chops over indirect heat until no longer pink inside, about 12 minutes per side. An instant-read thermometer should read at least 145 degrees F (63 degrees C). Allow chops to stand for 10 more minutes before serving.

BBQ Pork Chops

Ingredients:

1/2 cup barbecue sauce
3 tbsps. honey mustard
2 tsps. chopped fresh rosemary leaves
4 boneless pork loin chops, about 1 inch thick (about 1 lb)
1/4 tsp. salt
1/4 tsp. pepper

Directions:

1. Heat gas or charcoal grill. In small bowl, mix barbecue sauce, honey mustard and rosemary until well blended. Set aside.
2. Sprinkle both sides of pork chops with salt and pepper.
3. Place pork chops on grill over medium heat.
4. Cook 15 to 20 minutes, turning once or twice, until meat thermometer inserted in center reads 145 degrees F, brushing with barbecue sauce mixture during last 5 minutes of cook time.
5. In 1-quart saucepan, heat remaining barbecue sauce to boiling. Serve warm with pork chops.

Memphis Dry Rub Pork Chops

Sauce Ingredients:

1/2 cup ketchup
2 tbsps. molasses
1 tbsp. white wine vinegar
1 tbsp. Dijon mustard
1 tbsp. light brown sugar
2 tsps. Worcestershire sauce
1/2 tsp. kosher salt
1/4 tsp. Tabasco® sauce
1/4 tsp. granulated garlic
1/4 tsp. freshly ground black pepper

Rub Ingredients:

1 1/2 tsps. whole black peppercorns
1 1/2 tsps. mustard seed
1 1/2 tsps. paprika
1 1/2 tsps. light brown sugar
1 1/2 tsps. kosher salt
1 tsp. granulated garlic
1 tsp. granulated onion
1/4 tsp. ground cayenne pepper
6 bone-in pork rib chops, about 1" thick
Canola oil

Directions:

1. In a small heavy-bottom saucepan, whisk the sauce ingredients with 1/2 cup water.
2. Bring to boil over medium heat, then reduce the heat and simmer for 10 minutes, stirring occasionally.
3. In a spice grinder, pulse the peppercorns and the mustard seed until coarsely ground.
4. Place in a small bowl and add the remaining rub ingredients, mixing well.
5. Allow the chops to stand at room temperature for 20 to 30 minutes before grilling.
6. Lightly brush or spray the chops on both sides with oil and season with the rub, pressing the spices into the meat.
7. Grill over direct medium heat until barely pink in the center of the meat, 8 to 10 minutes, turning once.
8. Remove from the grill and let rest for 3 to 5 minutes. Serve warm with the sauce on the side.

North Carolina BBQ Pork Chops

Ingredients:

1.5 lbs. boneless pork chops

Rub Ingredients:

1 tbsp. dark brown sugar
1/2 tbsp. chili powder
1/2 tbsp. paprika
¾ tsp ground cumin
1/2 tsp. salt
1/2 tsp. pepper
Sprinkle of cayenne
Sauce ingredients:
1/3 cup ketchup
1/4 cup apple cider vinegar
2 tbsp. honey
2 tsp. Worcestershire

Directions:

1. Mix up all the ingredients for the spice rub in a small bowl.
2. Rub half all over the chops and let stand while you heat up the grill.
3. Wipe down the grill rack with cooking oil or non-stick spray.
4. Prepare the sauce, combining all ingredients in another small bowl, and set aside.
5. Before grilling, rub the remaining spice mixture on the chops.
6. Place on the grill for a total of about 5 minutes/side.
7. Cook time will vary depending on thickness and cut of meat.
8. Remove from heat and cover with foil while resting for about 5-10 minutes before serving.
9. Serve with the sauce.

Grilled Southwestern Pork Chops

Ingredients:

8 pork loin or rib chops, about 1/2 inch thick (about 2 lb)
1 tbsp. chili powder
1 tsp. ground cumin
1/4 tsp. ground red pepper (cayenne)
1/4 tsp. salt
1 large clove garlic, finely chopped

Directions:

1. In small bowl, mix all ingredients except pork; rub evenly on both sides of pork.
2. Cover; refrigerate 1 hour to blend flavors.
3. Heat gas or charcoal grill.
4. Place pork on grill.
5. Cover grill; cook over medium heat 8 to 10 minutes, turning frequently, until no longer pink in center.

Mexican Citrus Pork Chops With Mango Salsa

Ingredients:

1 large ripe mango, peeled, seeded and finely chopped
1/4 cup finely chopped red bell pepper
2 tbsps. orange juice
1 tbsp. chopped fresh cilantro
1/2 tsp. Mexican Seasoning
6 boneless pork chops
2 tbsps. Mexican seasoning

Directions:

1. For the Salsa, mix all ingredients in medium bowl until well blended.
2. Cover. Refrigerate until ready to serve.
3. For the Pork Chops, sprinkle pork chops with Seasoning.
4. Grill over medium heat 4 to 6 minutes per side or until desired doneness. Serve with Mango Salsa.

Baked Pork Chops

Peach-Glazed Pork Chops

Ingredients:

1 can (8-1/2 oz.) peach slices in juice, undrained   hot water
1/4 cup butter or margarine, cut up
1 pkg. (6 oz.) Stuffing Mix for Pork
6 bone-in pork chops, 1/2 inch thick
1/3 cup peach preserves

Directions:

1. Heat oven to 375 degrees F.
2. Drain peaches, reserving juice.
3. Add enough hot water to reserved juice to measure 1-1/2 cups; pour into large bowl.
4. Add butter and stir until melted.
5. Stir in stuffing mix and peaches. Let stand 5 min.
6. Spoon into 13x9-inch pan; top with chops.
7. Mix preserves and mustard; spoon over chops.
8. Bake 40 min. or until chops are done.

Parmesan-Crusted Pork Chops

Ingredients:

1 egg
1 tbsp. water
1/4 cup Italian style bread crumbs
1/3 cup grated Parmesan cheese
4 boneless pork loin chops, 3/4 inch thick
1 tbsp. olive oil

Directions:

1. Heat oven to 400 degrees F. Line 15x10x1-inch pan with foil; place cooling rack in pan.
2. In shallow bowl, beat egg and water with fork or whisk.
3. In another shallow bowl, stir bread crumbs and Parmesan cheese until well blended.
4. Dip each pork chop into egg mixture; coat with bread crumb mixture.
5. In 12-inch nonstick skillet, heat oil over medium-high heat.
6. Add pork chops; cook 1 to 2 minutes, turning once, until golden brown.
7. Place pork chops in pan.
8. Bake 13 to 18 minutes or until pork is no longer pink in center and meat thermometer inserted in center reads 145 degrees F.

Cola Pork Chops

Ingredients:

8 pork chops
1 cup cola-flavored carbonated beverage
1 cup ketchup
4 tbsps. brown sugar

Directions:

1. Preheat oven to 350 degrees F (175 degrees C).
2. Place pork chops in a 9x13 inch baking dish.
3. In a small bowl, mix together the cola and ketchup.
4. Pour over chops and sprinkle with brown sugar.
5. Bake uncovered for about 1 hour, or until pork is cooked through and internal temperature has reached 145 degrees F (63 degrees C).

Oven-Fried Pork Chops

Ingredients:

4 pork chops, trimmed
2 tbsps. butter, melted
1 egg, beaten
2 tbsps. milk
1/4 tsp. black pepper
1 cup herb-seasoned dry bread stuffing mix

Directions:

1. Preheat oven to 425 degrees F (220 degrees C).
2. Pour butter into a 9x13 inch baking pan.
3. Stir together egg, milk and pepper. Dip pork chops in egg mixture, coat with stuffing mix and place in pan.
4. Bake in preheated oven for 10 minutes. Turn chops and bake for another 10 minutes, or until no pink remains in the meat and juices run clear.

Crunchy Onion Pork Chops

Ingredients:

3 cup (6 oz.) crispy fried onions
3 tbsp. all-purpose flour
6 (1/2 inch) thick bone-in pork chops
1 large egg

Directions:

1. Place Crispy Fried Onions and flour into plastic bag.
2. Lightly crush with hands or with rolling pin. Transfer to pie plate or waxed paper.
3. Dip pork chops into beaten egg; then coat with onion crumbs, pressing firmly to adhere.
4. Place chops on baking sheet.
5. Bake at 400 degree F for 20 min. or until no longer pink in center.

Mexican Pork Chops

Ingredients:

1 tbsp. vegetable oil
4 boneless pork chops
2 (14.5 oz.) cans chopped stewed tomatoes, with juice
1 (8.75 oz.) can whole kernel corn, drained
1 (8 oz.) can red kidney beans, drained
1/2 cup uncooked long grain white rice
1 (4 oz.) can diced green chilies, drained
1/4 tsp. salt

Directions:

1. Preheat oven to 350 degrees F (175 degrees C).
2. Heat the oil in a skillet over medium heat. Brown the pork chops about 5 minutes on each side.
3. Remove chops from skillet and drain oil.
4. Mix the tomatoes, corn, kidney beans, rice, chilies, and salt into the skillet.
5. Bring liquid to a boil.
6. Cook and stir for 1 minute, until heated through. Transfer the tomato mixture to a baking dish.
7. Arrange the browned pork chops over the mixture.
8. Bake covered 30 minutes in the preheated oven. Uncover, and continue baking 10 minutes, until rice is tender and pork has reached an internal temperature of 145 degrees F (63 degrees C).

Taco Pork Chops

Ingredients:

6 pork chops
1 tsp. salt
3/4 cup uncooked rice
1/2-1 pkg. taco seasoning mix
1 can tomato sauce
1 1/2 cup water
1/2 cup shredded cheddar cheese
1 med. green pepper, cut into rings

Directions:

1. Brown pork chops.
2. Arrange in 9"x13"x2" baking dish.
3. Season with salt.
4. Sprinkle rice around chops.
5. Combine taco seasoning mix, tomato sauce and water; pour mixture over chops and rice.
6. Cover and bake at 350 degrees for 1 1/4 hours.
7. Remove from oven, sprinkle with cheese and arrange peppers over chops.
8. Cover and cook until cheese melts.

Pork Chops with Hard Cider

Ingredients:

2 tbsps. vegetable oil, divided
4 (1-inch thick) pork chops
2 cloves garlic, halved, or more to taste
1 large onion, sliced
1 cup uncooked white rice
2 apples - peeled, cored and sliced
2 1/2 cups chicken broth
1/2 cup hard cider
1/2 tsp. ground cloves
1 bay leaf
Salt and ground black pepper to taste

Directions:

1. Preheat oven to 350 degrees F (175 degrees C).
2. Heat 1 tbsp. oil in a large skillet over medium heat. Rub each pork chop on both sides with halved garlicup Add 2 pork chops to the skillet; cook until browned, 3 to 4 minutes per side. Transfer to a 4-quart casserole dish.
3. Repeat with remaining 2 pork chops.
4. Heat remaining 1 tbsp. oil in the same skillet.
5. Add onion; cook and stir until softened, about 5 minutes.
6. Add to pork chops in the casserole dish.
7. Spread rice and apples on top.
8. Combine chicken broth, hard cider, cloves, bay leaf, salt, and black pepper in a 1-quart saucepan; bring to a boil.
9. Pour broth mixture over apples in the casserole dish.
10. Cover with aluminum foil.
11. Bake in the preheated oven until an instant-read thermometer inserted into the pork chops reads 145 degrees F (63 degrees C), about 45 minutes.

Horseradish Pork Chops

Ingredients:

4 boneless pork chops
1/4 cup melted butter
1/4 cup dry bread crumbs
1/4 cup prepared horseradish

Directions:

1. Preheat oven to 350 degrees F (175 degrees C).
2. Grease a 9x13-inch baking dish.
3. Place the pork chops into the prepared baking dish.
4. Mix together the butter, bread crumbs, and horseradish. Spoon the mixture onto the pork chops, and press down the mixture to completely coat each chop with about 1/4 of the mixture.
5. Bake in the preheated oven until the chops are tender, about 45 minutes.

Orange Ginger Pork Chops

Ingredients:

1/4 cup all-purpose flour
2 tsps. ground ginger
Salt to taste
1/2 tsp. ground black pepper
4 tbsps. olive oil
4 thick cut pork chops
1 onion, halved and thinly sliced
1 tbsp. brandy
1 1/2 cups orange juice

Directions:

1. Preheat the oven to 350 degrees F (175 degrees C).
2. Place the flour, ginger, salt and pepper into a paper or plastic bag. Put the chops in the bag, and shake to coat. Heat oil in a frying pan over medium-high heat. Brown pork chops in the hot oil on both sides. Transfer the chops to a casserole dish.
3. Place the onion in the hot frying pan, and cook until limp.
4. Pour the brandy into the pan, and stir to incorporate any bits of food that may be stuck to the pan.
5. Pour the onion and juices over the pork chops in the dish.
6. Pour the orange juice into the casserole as well.
7. Cover and bake for 45 minutes, or until chops are no longer pink. Serve with the orange sauce from the dish.

Pork Chop and Cheesy Rice Casserole

Ingredients:

1 (16 oz.) can chicken broth
1 1/2 cups rice
1 (10 oz.) can cream of chicken soup
1 cup water
4 oz. shredded Cheddar cheese
1 pound boneless pork chops
Salt and ground black pepper to taste

Directions:

1. Preheat oven to 350 degrees F (175 degrees C).
2. Grease a 3-quart casserole dish.
3. Stir chicken broth, rice, cream of chicken soup, and water together with a whisk in the prepared casserole dish until smooth; add Cheddar cheese, season with salt and pepper, and stir.
4. Lie pork chops into the rice mixture in a single layer; season with more black pepper.
5. Bake in preheated oven until rice in the middle of the dish is tender and pork chops are golden brown, about 80 minutes.

Lemony Pork Piccata

Ingredients:

4 pork chops
1/2 cup all-purpose flour
Salt and ground black pepper to taste
3 tbsps. unsalted butter
2 tbsps. sliced shallots
1/3 cup dry white wine
1/4 cup chicken stock
1 tbsp. fresh lemon juice
1/4 cup chopped fresh parsley
1 tbsp. lemon zest
1 tbsp. capers

Directions:

1. Preheat oven to 300 degrees F (150 degrees C).
2. Pound pork chops between 2 sheets waxed paper or plastic wrap until very thin, about 1/8 inch.
3. Mix flour, salt, and pepper together in a shallow bowl. Dredge both sides of each pork chop through flour mixture, shaking off any excess flour.
4. Heat butter in a large skillet over medium heat until butter starts to sizzle.
5. Add shallots and pork chops in 1 layer, working in batches if needed.
6. Cook pork chops until golden brown and almost cooked through, 3 to 4 minutes per side. Transfer pork chops to a baking dish and lightly tent with aluminum foil, reserving the shallots and browned bits of food in the skillet.
7. Bake pork chops in the preheated oven until cooked through, 20 to 25 minutes. An instant-read thermometer inserted into the center should read at least 145 degrees F (63 degrees C).
8. Pour wine and chicken stock into the skillet and bring to a boil while scraping the browned bits of food off of the bottom with a wooden spoon.
9. Reduce heat and simmer until sauce is reduced by half, 2 to 5 minutes.
10. Stir lemon juice into sauce.
11. Drizzle sauce over pork chops and top with parsley, lemon zest, and capers.

Peachy Tender Pork Chops

Ingredients:

1 (29 oz.) can peach halves
8 pork chops, 1/2 inch thick
1 env. Shake and Bake for pork
1/4 cup packed brown sugar
1/4 cup ketchup
2 tbsp. vinegar

Directions:

1. Drain peaches; reserve syrup. Moisten chops in 1/4 cup of syrup. Coat chops with mix.
2. Arrange in single layer on rack in ungreased, shallow baking pan.
3. Bake at 425 degrees F for 40 minutes.
4. Place peaches in pan with chops. Brush with peach syrup and bake 5 to 10 minutes longer or until chops are tender.
5. Meanwhile, heat together 1/2 cup peach syrup, the brown sugar, ketchup, and vinegar.
6. Serve with chops and peaches.

Honey Dijon Pork Chops

Ingredients:

1/4 cup Dijon mustard
1/4 cup honey
1 tsp. ground black pepper
1 tsp. garlic powder
4 boneless pork loin chops

Directions:

1. Preheat oven to 350 degrees F (175 degrees C).
2. Grease a baking dish.
3. Mix Dijon mustard, honey, black pepper, and garlic powder in a bowl.
4. Arrange pork chops in prepared baking dish and pour mustard mixture over pork.
5. Bake in preheated oven until pork is slightly pink in the center, about 45 minutes. An instant-read thermometer inserted into the center should read at least 145 degrees F (63 degrees C).

Graham Crusted Pork Chops

Ingredients:

4 thick cut pork chops
2 cups graham cracker crumbs
1 tsp. ground cinnamon
1 tsp. curry powder
1/2 tsp. dried rosemary
1/2 tsp. salt
1/2 tsp. ground black pepper
1 egg, beaten

Directions:

1. Preheat an oven to 375 degrees F (190 degrees C).
2. Rinse the pork chops and pat dry.
3. Combine graham cracker crumbs, cinnamon, curry powder, rosemary, salt, and pepper in a large resealable plastic bag. Dip the pork chops in the egg and place in plastic bag; shake to coat.
4. Place the pork chops in a prepared 9 x 13 inch baking dish.
5. Bake until the pork is no longer pink in the center, about 40 minutes. An instant-read thermometer inserted into the center should read 145 degrees F (63 degrees C).

Pecan Crusted Pork Chops

Ingredients:

2 cups pecans
1 tsp. salt
1/4 tsp. freshly ground black pepper
1/2 cup all-purpose flour
3 eggs
6 (1 inch thick) pork chops
3 tbsps. unsalted butter
Italian flat leaf parsley

Directions:

1. Preheat an oven to 350 degrees F (175 degrees C).
2. Spread the pecans on a baking sheet, and bake until lightly toasted, about 5 minutes. Set pecans aside to cool. Raise the oven temperature to 375 degrees (190 degrees C).
3. Chop pecans finely, and then combine in a shallow bowl with the salt and pepper.
4. Place the flour in another shallow bowl.
5. In a third bowl, whisk the eggs together until well blended. First dip each pork chop into the flour, shaking off any excess.
6. Then dip the chops into the egg, and finally into the finely chopped pecans.
7. In a large oven-proof frying pan, melt the butter over a medium heat.
8. Arrange the pork chops in a single layer in the pan.
9. Cook, turning once, until golden on both sides, 5 to 6 minutes total.
10. Place the frying pan in the preheated oven, and bake until firm to the touch and pale pink when cut in the center, about 10 to 12 minutes.
11. Do not allow the nut coating to burn. Transfer the pork chops to a warmed platter, and garnish with parsley sprigs. Serve and enjoy!

Italian Breaded Pork Chops

Ingredients:

3 eggs, lightly beaten
3 tbsps. milk
1 1/2 cups Italian seasoned bread crumbs
1/2 cup grated Parmesan cheese
2 tbsps. dried parsley
2 tbsps. olive oil
4 cloves garlic, peeled and chopped
4 pork chops

Directions:

1. Preheat oven to 325 degrees F (160 degrees C).
2. In a small bowl, beat together the eggs and milk.
3. In a separate small bowl, mix the bread crumbs, Parmesan cheese, and parsley.
4. Heat the olive oil in a large, oven-proof skillet over medium heat.
5. Stir in the garlic, and cook until lightly browned.
6. Remove garlic, reserving for other uses.
7. Dip each pork chop into the egg mixture, then into the bread crumb mixture, coating evenly.
8. Place coated pork chops in the skillet, and brown abut 5 minutes on each side.
9. Place the skillet and pork chops in the preheated oven, and cook 25 minutes, or to an internal temperature of 145 degrees F (63 degrees C).

Sweet And Sour Pork Chops

Ingredients:

3 lbs. pork chops
4 onions, diced
1 can pineapple chunks
1/2 cup vinegar
1/2 cup brown sugar
4 tbsps. soy sauce
1/2 tsp. freshly grated ginger
1/4 cup cornstarch
1 1/2 cups water
1 can water chestnuts
1 green bell pepper
salt and pepper, to taste
In a Dutch oven or large skillet, brown the pork chops.
Add onions, juice from the pineapple, vinegar, soy sauce, sugar, ginger, salt and pepper.
Cover pan and simmer for 1 hour or until pork chops are tender.
Set pork chops aside.

Directions:

1. Combine cornstarch and water, then stir into pan; add water chestnuts, bell pepper, and chunks of pineapple.
2. Bring to a boil and cook until sauce has thickened to desired consistency
3. Add pork chops and cook until heated through.
4. Serve over white rice, pasta, or noodles.

Onion Soup Pork Chops

Ingredients:

2 pork chops
1 (1 oz.) package dry onion soup mix
1 (6 oz.) package uncooked wild rice
3 cups water

Directions:

1. Preheat oven to 350 degrees F (175 degrees C).
2. Brown pork chops in a medium skillet over medium heat.
3. In a medium bowl combine the soup mix and rice.
4. Mix together and spread in the bottom of a 9x13 inch baking dish. Lay browned chops on top of rice.
5. Pour water over all, gently.
6. Cover dish tightly with aluminum foil and bake in the preheated oven for 1 hour, or until internal temperature of the pork has reached 145 degrees F (63 degrees C).

Lemon Baked Pork Chops

Ingredients:

6 pork chops
2 tbsp. all-purpose flour
1/2 tsp. salt
1/4 tsp. pepper
1 tbsp. shortening
3/4 cup ketchup
3/4 cup water
3 tbsp. brown sugar
6 slices lemon

Directions:

1. Sprinkle pork chops with salt and pepper; dip in flour and brown both sides in skillet. Transfer to baking dish with lemon slice on each pork chop.
2. Mix ketchup, water and sugar and pour over chops.
3. Bake uncovered for 45 minutes at 350 degrees F.

Chili Powder Baked Pork Chops

Ingredients:

6-8 center cut pork chops
chili powder
salt and pepper, to taste

Directions:

1. Wash the pork chops then salt and pepper both sides. Layer them in an oblong Pyrex or bakeware dish that has been sprayed with Pam.
2. Sprinkle the top side of the pork chops with chili powder.
3. Cover securely with foil and bake 1 hour in 350 degrees F. oven.
4. Serve them with rice and green beans.

Lemon Pepper Marinated Pork Chops

Ingredients:

6 pork chops
2 tbsps. lemon pepper
2 tsps. apple cider vinegar
1/2 cup vegetable oil
1 1/2 cups water

Directions:

1. In a stainless steel pan or ceramic baking dish, whisk together 2 tbsps. Lawry's lemon pepper seasoning, 2 tsps. of apple cider vinegar, 1/2 cup vegetable oil, and 1 1/2 cups water.
2. Place pork chops in the marinade and marinate for 30 to 45 minutes in refrigerator, turning once or twice.
3. Remove from refrigerator and pour out marinade.
4. Cover with foil.
5. Bake at 375 degrees F for about 1 hour (more of less according to thickness) and serve.

Potato Tomato Pork Chop Bake

Ingredients:

4 or 6 loin pork chops
4 or 5 medium size potatoes
3 medium onions
2 tbsp. oil
1 clove garlic
1/4 tsp. oregano
1 small can tomato paste
Salt and pepper to taste

Directions:

1. In bottom of glass baking dish or pan, put 2 tbsps. oil, clove of garlic, cut in quarters and oregano.
2. Pour in can of tomato paste.
3. Pare and cut potatoes into medium chunks.
4. Line the bottom of pan.
5. Cut onions into medium slices and place over potatoes.
6. Line pork chops over onions.
7. Top each chop with a small piece of garlic, fresh bread crumbs, parsley, oregano, salt and pepper to taste.
8. Pour hot water in baking dish (to reach but not cover pork chops).
9. Place single sheet of aluminum foil over pan. (Do not tuck around pan.)
10. Bake in 350 degree oven for 1 hour or until chops are done.
11. Pan should simmer slowly so water does not spill over.

Pork Chop Potato and Carrot Bake

Ingredients:

Pork chops
Potatoes, peeled and cut in to wedges
Carrots, peeled and cut in to 1 to 2 inch pieces
Salt and pepper
Butter
Onion, peeled and sliced
Worcestershire sauce

Directions:

1. Preheat the oven to 375 degrees F.
2. Lay 1 pork chop in the center of a large piece of foil.
3. Top with a heaping handful of potatoes and carrots.
4. Add several slices of onion, dab of butter, salt and pepper and Worcestershire sauce to taste.
5. Fold foil by crimping top and sides to seal tightly.
6. Lay on a cookie sheet.
7. Repeat with as many pork chops as needed.
8. Place the cookie sheet in the oven and bake for 1 hour.
9. If large or thick pork chops are used, bake 15 to 20 minutes longer.

German Pork Chops

Ingredients:

16 oz. sauerkraut
1 (15 oz.) jar applesauce
1 tbsp. brown sugar
6 (1" thick) pork chops
1/2 tsp. dried sage
1 tbsp. Vegetable oil
2 tbsp. Lemon
1/4 cup water

Directions:

1. Preheat oven to 375 degrees F.
2. Grease a medium baking dish.
3. Rinse sauerkraut and drain it.
4. Combine sauerkraut, applesauce and brown sugar in a medium bowl.
5. Mix well.
6. Spoon in to a prepared baking dish.
7. Rub pork with sage.
8. Heat oil in a large skillet over medium high heat.
9. Cook pork chops, turning once, until browned (about 2 minutes per side).
10. Arrange pork over sauerkraut mixture.
11. Pour lemon juice and water over pork.
12. Bake, covered with foil for about 30 minutes or until pork is tender.

Ranch Pork Chops

Ingredients:

1 packet (1 oz.) ranch salad dressing mix
6 pork chops about 1-inch thick
Dash of paprika
Salt
Fresh cracked black pepper

Directions:

1. Preheat the oven to 450 degrees F.
2. In a small bowl, add the ranch salad dressing mix, together with the salt, pepper, and paprika and mix well.
3. Liberally sprinkle the pork chops on both sides with the salad dressing mixture.
4. Arrange the chops on a baking sheet.
5. Bake the pork chops for 20 minutes, turning once until browned.
6. Serve immediately.
7. Enjoy!

About the Author

Laura Sommers is **The Recipe Lady!**

She is a loving wife and mother who lives on a small farm in Baltimore County, Maryland and has a passion for all things domestic especially when it comes to saving money. She has a profitable eBay business and is a couponing addict. Follow her tips and tricks to learn how to make delicious meals on a budget, save money or to learn the latest life hack!

Visit the Recipe Lady's blog for even more great recipes:

http://the-recipe-lady.blogspot.com/

Follow her on Pinterest:

http://pinterest.com/therecipelady1

Other Books by Laura Sommers

Egg Salad Recipes

The Chip Dip Cookbook

Zucchini Recipes

Salsa recipes

Traditional Vermont Recipes

Recipe Hacks for Dry Onion Soup Mix

Made in the USA
Middletown, DE
04 February 2020